D1473262

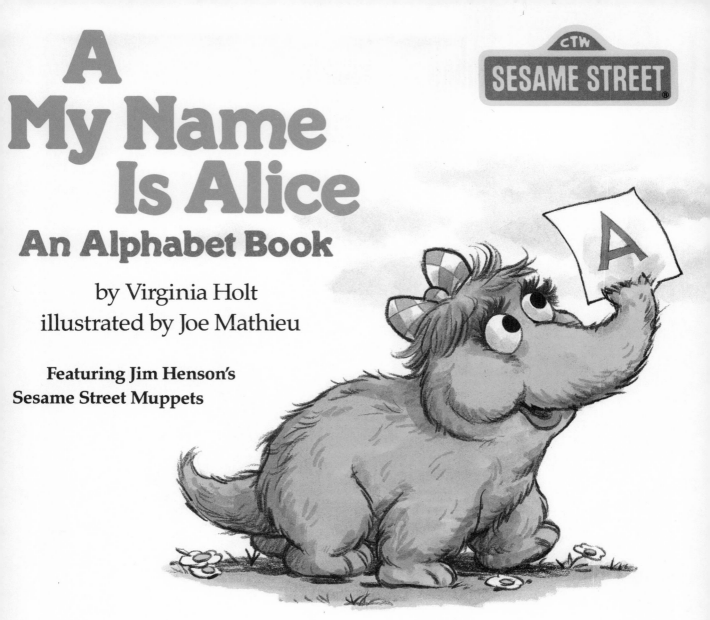

CTW
SESAME STREET®

A My Name Is Alice

An Alphabet Book

by Virginia Holt
illustrated by Joe Mathieu

**Featuring Jim Henson's
Sesame Street Muppets**

A Random House PICTUREBACK®

Random House/Children's Television Workshop

Copyright © 1989 Children's Television Workshop. Sesame Street MUPPETS © Muppets, Inc. 1989. All rights reserved under International and Pan-American Copyright Conventions. ® Sesame Street and the Sesame Street sign are trademarks and service marks of the Children's Television Workshop. Published in the United States by Random House, Inc., New York, and simultaneously in Canada by Random House of Canada Limited, Toronto, in conjunction with the Children's Television Workshop.

Library of Congress Cataloging-in-Publication Data:
Holt, Virginia. A my name is Alice : a Sesame Street alphabet book / by Virginia Holt.   p.   cm.–(A Random House pictureback) SUMMARY: The Muppets introduce the alphabet with short poems about dinosaurs, cookies, ladders, quilts, and zebras. ISBN: 0-394-82241-2 (pbk.); 0-394-92241-7 (lib. bdg.) 1. English language–Alphabet–Juvenile literature. 2. Children's poetry, American. [1. Alphabet. 2. American poetry] I. Title. II. Title: Sesame Street alphabet book. III. Series.   PE1155.H64   1989   421'.54–dc19   [E]   88-18520

Manufactured in the United States of America   1 2 3 4 5 6 7 8 9 0

Aa

A my name is Alice,
and my brother's Aloysius.
My favorite food is apples,
and I think they are delicious.

Bb

B my name is Bert,
and I love to throw my ball.
I take turns with my buddy
as we bounce it off the wall.

Cc

C my name is Cookie,
and me tell you, chocolate chips
are my very favorite cookies!
Oh, they make me smack my lips!

Dd

D this is a dinosaur
that's called Tyrannosaurus.
He doesn't live here anymore
but left his bones here for us.

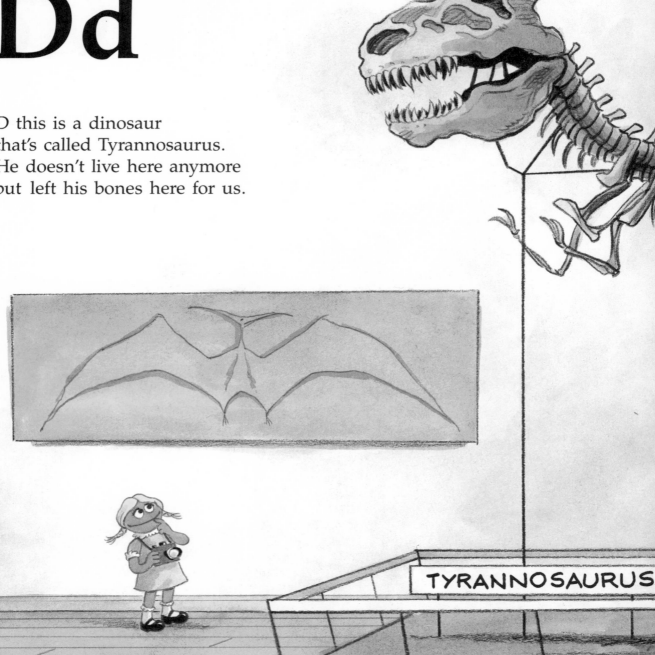

TYRANNOSAURUS

Ee

E my name is Ernie,
and this is my little ear.
I bet you have a set yourself.
That's how we both can hear.

Ff

F I found a feather!
It was floating in the air.
Do you think it could belong
to that big bird over there?

Gg

G my name is Grover,
and this white bird is a goose.
I have to run and grab it
if it happens to get loose.

Hh

H my name is Herry,
and this animal's a horse.
I give him lots of hay, yah,
at feeding time, of course.

Ii

I this is an iceberg.
It's an island made of ice.
For me it's kind of chilly
but these penguins think it's nice.

Jj

J my jellybeans are
in a jar high on the shelf.
If I stand up on this footstool,
I can reach them by myself.

Kk

K this is a keyhole,
and this shiny thing's a key.
The key fits in the keyhole
and unlocks the lock for me.

L this is my ladder,
and it helps me to climb high.
I need to change these light bulbs.
Can you guess the reason why?

Mm

M my name is Mumford,
and this is a magic trick.
I will now change this mud to milk.
It didn't work? Oh, ick!

N it is my nap time,
so I'm going to my nest.
I've played so hard all morning
that I need to take a rest.

Oo

O I am an ostrich.
I am so tall and grand.
When I want to hide myself
my head goes in the sand.

Pp

P I'm Prairie Dawn,
and I'm printing with this press
on a roll of clean white paper
secret numbers. Can you guess?

Qq

Q this is my quilt,
and I keep it on my bed.
It makes me feel quite snuggy
from my toes up to my head.

Rr

R I'm Rodeo Rosie,
and I love to play outside
on the ranch where I was reared
and learned to rope and ride.

Ss

S these are my seashells,
and I found them at the shore.
I love to sit and count them.
Splendid! Nothing thrills me more!

Tt

T this is a train,
and it runs upon a track.
Its whistle goes *woo-woo-woo*
and its wheels go *clicky-clack.*

Uu

U my new umbrella
is so good. Do you know why?
It's big enough to keep
all my friends completely dry.

Vv

V for valentines to make,
and when you are all through,
the fun is giving them away.
I made one just for you!

Ww

W for wagon,
it's a thing with wheels you pull.
It is easy when it's empty,
but it's harder when it's full.

Xx

X this is an x-ray—
a look at what's inside.
When you have an x-ray taken,
there is little you can hide.

Y this is a yo-yo,
and it is my favorite thing,
except that every time I try it,
I get tangled in the string.

Yy

Z z

Z this is a zebra—
if you said so, you were right.
Are the white stripes on the black,
or the black stripes on the white?

Now you know the alphabet—
the letters A to Z.
If you want to say it all again,
go back to A with me.